KEEP
CALM
AND
PEDAL
ON

KEEP CALM AND PEDAL ON

EBURY
PRESS

3 5 7 9 10 8 6 4

Published in 2014 by Ebury Press, an imprint of Ebury Publishing

A Random House Group Company

Text and design © Ebury Press 2014

The Random House Group Limited Reg. No. 954009

Addresses for companies within the Random House Group can be
found at www.randomhouse.co.uk

A CIP catalogue record for this book is available from the British Library

To buy books by your favourite authors and register for
offers visit www.randomhouse.co.uk

Printed and bound by TBB, a.s. (Slovakia)
Text compiled by Jonathan Swan
Designed by Lucy Stephens
Edited by Ian Preece and Laura Nickoll

ISBN 9780091957797

LIFE IS LIKE RIDING A BICYCLE – IN ORDER TO KEEP YOUR BALANCE, YOU MUST KEEP MOVING.

ALBERT EINSTEIN

CONTENTS

INTRODUCTION

Which childhood toy is the one that most people can remember? Their first bike. In fact, a surprising number of people, many of whom can't recall the date of their own mother's birthday, possess an uncanny recall of the whole fleet of bicycles that came their way: the yellow one, then the red racer, the black BMX. Proust may have had his madeleines, but go to a park on any given Saturday and the sight of a small child wobbling along, Dad gamely scuttling behind holding the saddle, will spontaneously trigger reminiscences in all who survey the scene. Cycling bites early, and it bites deep.

What does the bike offer that elevates it so far above other childhood playthings? Could it be that the bike isn't really a toy in the first place? Or rather, it is the supreme toy that offers so much more than any other one could hope to manage. It promises freedom, independence, speed, exploration . . . the opening up of new horizons and possibilities. It expands the world. And when other childish things have been put away, the bike alone retains its appeal and allure.

Riding a bike is popular right now. An Englishman has even won the Tour de France, a feat that would have seemed improbable only a decade ago. Read any of the latest cycling autobiographies of professional cyclists such as David Millar and Charly Wegelius and you get the picture that until relatively recently, cycling just wasn't taken seriously over here. Instead it was an opaque sport that happened over on 'the Continent'. Conceptually, bicycle racing was viewed rather like a bidet: distinctly foreign and mysterious in its workings. It's all different now. Exotic sanitary-ware is available in B&Q, and cyclists have become household names: Wiggo has entered the lexicon and Victoria Pendleton has entered *Strictly Come Dancing*.

But bike riding isn't just a pursuit for children, racers ('scorchers' the Victorians called them, thinking cycle speedsters a thoroughly bad lot) and wealthy middle-aged men having a mid-life crisis. As the quotes in this book show, the bike means all sorts of things to different people. The benefits of biking from an environmental point of view aren't just about cutting down on car use and reducing pollution; cyclists also point to the connection that is made with the natural world when out for a ride. A healthy mind, in a healthy body, perched on a well-sprung saddle with the wind at your back, is the recipe for happiness. And it would seem that cyclists really do have the wind with them. Consider, for example, the Boris-Bike in London, the Vélib in Paris, the citi-bike in New York, and countless other cycle-hire schemes. These all work because people want to use them: the best way to get around a modern city isn't in a car. It's on a bike.

Of course, going cycling isn't all downhill, through rustic countryside in sunny weather. There's quite a lot of going uphill. Cyclists are connoisseurs of pain, talking about it in a way that is almost reverential; and no pain is as sanctified as the pain of a cyclist who is turning himself inside out climbing a big mountain, every pedal stroke a torture. When a cyclist can't keep up with the race as it climbs, he cracks, often suddenly and spectacularly.

In the Tour de France, it's the mountains that are the most eagerly anticipated stages, and the names of the most forbidding and testing are mythical: Alpe d'Huez, Mount Ventoux, Col du Galibier, Col du Tourmalet.

But for most of us, cycling in the Alps isn't in our immediate plans, although it may be in our minds more than we would care to admit. When a cycling commuter toils up a hill on his way home from work, he may look a sorry assortment of flapping mudguards and wonky helmet. But, who knows? In his mind's eye, he is bursting clear of the pack, the road winding clear before him, up to the peak of the mountain and the finish line and the cheering crowds.

A lot of hopes and dreams are perched on the slender frame of the bicycle. But, as these quotes show, it is more than able to carry them, and more. So mount up, keep calm and pedal on!

THE
DAWN OF
CYCLING

SLIDING DOWN A
HILL ON A HANDSAW
WOULD BE TWO
DEGREES MORE
COMFORTABLE THAN
EXPERIMENTING
ON ONE OF THESE
CONTRIVANCES.

UNKNOWN

FOR THE MAJORITY OF CIVILIZED HUMANITY, WALKING IS ON ITS LAST LEGS.

SCIENTIFIC AMERICAN,
1869

THE PERFECTION OF THE BICYCLE WAS THE GREATEST INCIDENT OF THE NINETEENTH CENTURY.

UNKNOWN

THE NOTHING
OF THE DAY IS A
MACHINE CALLED THE
VELOCIPEDE. IT IS A
WHEEL CARRIAGE TO
RIDE COCK-HORSE
UPON, SITTING ASTRIDE
AND PUSHING IT ALONG
WITH THE TOES.

JOHN KEATS,
1819

A DANDY, ON
A VELOCIPEDE

I SAW IN A
VISION SWEET

ALONG THE HIGHWAY
MAKING SPEED

WITH HIS
ALTERNATE FEET.

*BLACKWOOD'S
MAGAZINE,*
1871

COMING DOWNHILL IS WARRANTED TO KILL NINE AND THREE-SIXTEENTHS TIMES OUT OF 10.

'THE COLUMBIAD',
1807

HORSES, IT MUST BE ADMITTED, DO NOT LIKE BICYCLES.

THE TIMES,
1878

BICYCLISTS HAVE BECOME A POWER.

THE TIMES,
1870

EARLY ATTITUDES

VELOCIPEDISTS ARE IMBECILES ON WHEELS!

LE GAULOIS,
1869

PHYSICALLY, MORALLY AND SOCIALLY, THE BENEFITS CYCLING CONFERS ARE ALMOST UNBOUNDED.

A. W. RUMNE,
1936

SOMETIMES, 'TIS TRUE,
I AM A TOY,

CONTRIVED TO PLEASE
SOME ACTIVE BOY;

BUT I AMUSE EACH
JACK O'DANDY,

E'EN GREAT MEN
SOMETIMES HAVE
ME HANDY,

WHO, WHEN ON ME
GET ASTRIDE

THINK THAT ON
PEGASUS THEY RIDE.

ANON

BICYCLING IS A HEALTHY AND MANLY PURSUIT AND, UNLIKE OTHER FOOLISH CRAZES, IT HAS NOT DIED OUT.

DAILY TELEGRAPH,
1877

NEWSPAPERS ARE SEEMINGLY UNABLE TO DISCRIMINATE BETWEEN A BICYCLE ACCIDENT AND THE COLLAPSE OF CIVILISATION.

GEORGE BERNARD SHAW

TWO REASONS TO REFUSE TO TASTE VELOCIPEDIC DELIGHTS: POVERTY AND PILES.

BAUDRY DE SAUNIER,
1891

THERE IS SOMETHING UNCANNY IN THE NOISELESS RUSH OF THE CYCLIST.

POPULAR SCIENCE,
1891

THE CLAIM THAT THE SUNDAY BICYCLING CROWDS ARE NOISY, BOISTEROUS, PROFANE, ETC., HAS SOME FOUNDATION IN FACT.

DR VICTOR NEESEN,
1872

LEARNING
TO RIDE

THE AVERAGE PERSON CAN LEARN THE BICYCLE IN SIX MONTHS, PROVIDED THEY DON'T MISS A SINGLE DAY.

JEROME K. JEROME,
1900

I DON'T KNOW WHY I LIKE IT.

LEO TOLSTOY

I LEARNED TO RIDE MY BICYCLE UPON SANDY TRACKS WITH NO ONE BUT GOD TO HELP ME.

H. G. WELLS,
1934

A SHAKY CHILD ON A BICYCLE FOR THE FIRST TIME NEEDS BOTH SUPPORT AND FREEDOM. THE REALISATION THAT THIS IS WHAT THE CHILD WILL ALWAYS NEED CAN HIT HARD.

SLOAN WILSON

LEARN TO RIDE A BICYCLE. YOU WILL NOT REGRET IT, IF YOU LIVE.

MARK TWAIN

ONE OF THE MOST IMPORTANT DAYS OF MY LIFE WAS WHEN I LEARNED TO RIDE A BICYCLE.

MICHAEL PALIN

DIFFERENT (PEDAL) STROKES

SHARING A BED IS REALLY NOTHING COMPARED WITH SHARING A TANDEM.

A. A. MILNE

THE SLOWER YOU GO THE MORE LIKELY IT IS YOU'LL CRASH.

JULI FURTADO

IF YOU WANNA
TAKE A NAP, LIE
DOWN. IF YOU WANNA
RIDE A BIKE, BUY A
F****** BICYCLE.

GEORGE CARLIN

MECHANICS,
DAY-LABOURERS,
CHIMNEY-SWEEPS,
COSTERS, ETC., WHO
ARE NOW HAILED AS
MEN AND BROTHERS
IN BICYCLE CONTESTS,
SHALL NEVER FIND A
PLACE IN THE NATIONAL
TRICYCLE ASSOCIATION.

BICYCLING NEWS,
1878

A MOUNTAIN BIKE IS LIKE YOUR BUDDY. A ROAD BIKE IS YOUR LOVER.

SEAN COFFEY

SHRED LIGHTLY.

SCOT NICOL

**AT ITS BEST,
MOUNTAIN BIKING
IS EVEN BIGGER THAN
THE MOUNTAIN.**

BILL STRICKLAND

ROAD RACING MADE MOUNTAIN BIKING SEEM CHILDISH AND TRANSIENT.

DAVID MILLAR

CHILDHOOD

EVERY TIME YOU MISS YOUR CHILDHOOD, RIDE ON A BICYCLE!

MEHMET MURAT ILDAN

WHEN I WAS A KID
I USED TO PRAY EVERY
NIGHT FOR A NEW
BICYCLE. THEN I
REALISED THAT THE
LORD DOESN'T WORK
THAT WAY SO I STOLE
ONE AND ASKED HIM
TO FORGIVE ME.

EMO PHILIPS

OH, ALL YE GAY AND
FESTIVE YOUTH,

REMEMBER MY
ADVIC-ICAL,

AND HASTE TO PROVE
THIS PRECIOUS TRUTH –

THERE'S NOTHING
LIKE THE BICYCLE.

WALTER PARKE,
1874

A CHILDHOOD WITHOUT A BICYCLE IS A SAILBOAT BECALMED.

JAMES E. STARRS

WOMEN
ON TWO
WHEELS

SHE WHO SUCCEEDS IN GAINING THE MASTERY WILL GAIN THE MASTERY OF LIFE.

FRANCES E. WILLARD,
1895

THE BICYCLE IS JUST
AS GOOD COMPANY
AS MOST HUSBANDS.
WHEN IT GETS
OLD AND SHABBY,
A WOMAN CAN
DISPOSE OF IT AND
GET A NEW ONE
WITHOUT SHOCKING
THE ENTIRE
COMMUNITY.

ANN STRONG,
Minneapolis Tribune,
1895

THERE IS A TYPE OF WOMAN WHO SHOULD NEVER ASSUME THE BICYCLING POSTURE.

P. J. O'ROURKE

IN YOUNG GIRLS
THE BONES OF
THE PELVIS ARE
NOT ABLE TO RESIST
THE TENSION
REQUIRED TO RIDE
A BICYCLE, AND
SO MAY BECOME
DISTORTED
IN SHAPE.

NORTHERN WHEELER,
1892

A WOMAN
NEEDS A MAN
LIKE A FISH NEEDS
A BICYCLE.

IRINA DUNN

IT HAS DONE MORE
TO EMANCIPATE
WOMEN THAN
ANYTHING ELSE IN
THE WORLD.
I STAND AND REJOICE
EVERY TIME I SEE A
WOMAN RIDE BY ON
A WHEEL.

SUSAN B. ANTHONY,
1896

THE HOUSEMAID
AND THE COOK ARE
BOTH A-RIDING ON
THEIR WHEELS;

AND DADDY'S IN THE
KITCHEN A-COOKING
OF THE MEALS.

FLORA THOMPSON,
1939

CYCLISTS
AT LARGE

THE BEST RIDES ARE THE ONES WHERE YOU BITE OFF MUCH MORE THAN YOU CAN CHEW, AND LIVE THROUGH IT.

DOUG BRADBURY

LIKE DOGS, BICYCLES ARE SOCIAL CATALYSTS THAT ATTRACT A SUPERIOR CATEGORY OF PEOPLE.

CHIP BROWN

THIS IS THE PARADOX AT THE HEART OF CYCLING: TO COMPETE, EVEN RIVALS MUST CO-OPERATE.

MATT RENDELL

BICYCLES HAVE THEIR PROPER PLACE: UNDER SMALL BOYS DELIVERING EVENING PAPERS.

P. J. O'ROURKE

AS MID-LIFE
CRISES GO,
DRESSING UP
IN SPANDEX
AND PRETENDING
YOU'RE IN
THE TOUR DE
FRANCE SEEMS A
PRETTY BENIGN
DELUSION.

MATT SEATON

IT IS NOT ONLY
THAT I BELONG TO
THAT PATHETIC AND
DWINDLING MINORITY
OF WHITE, MARRIED,
OLD ETONIAN
MODERATE SMOKERS
AND DRINKERS. THIS
ADMISSION IS FAR
WORSE. MY FRIENDS,
I AM A CYCLIST.

BORIS JOHNSON

PHILOSOPHICAL CYCLING

IF AT ANY POINT
BETWEEN THE
BEGINNING AND THE
END OF HIS JOURNEY
HE STOPS MOVING, HE
WILL FALL OFF IT. THAT
IS A METAPHOR FOR A
MAN'S JOURNEY
THROUGH LIFE.

WILLIAM GOLDING

DEATH MAY
HAVE NO MASTER,
BUT THE BICYCLE IS,
MOST EMPHATICALLY,
NOT ITS SLAVE.

JAMES E. STARRS

CYCLING IS LIKE A CHURCH – MANY ATTEND, BUT FEW UNDERSTAND.

JIM BURLANT

LIFE IS LIKE
A 10-SPEED BICYCLE.
MOST OF US
HAVE GEARS WE
NEVER USE.

CHARLES SCHULTZ

IF THE
CONSTELLATIONS
HAD BEEN NAMED
IN THE TWENTIETH
CENTURY, I SUPPOSE
WE WOULD SEE
BICYCLES.

CARL SAGAN

**CYCLING IS FREE,
IT IS OUTSIDE, IT
IS THE WEATHER,
IT IS THE PLANET,
IT IS ENERGY.**

RALF HÜTTER

WHEN MAN INVENTED THE BICYCLE HE REACHED THE PEAK OF HIS ATTAINMENTS.

ELIZABETH WEST

TO ATTACK THE PEDALS MAY BE STRENUOUS BUT IT IS AN EXPRESSION OF TRUST IN ONE'S OWN POWERS.

WOLFGANG SACHS

CYCLING: GOOD FOR THE MIND

GIVE A MAN A FISH AND
FEED HIM FOR A DAY.
TEACH A MAN TO FISH
AND FEED HIM FOR A
LIFETIME. TEACH A MAN
TO CYCLE AND HE WILL
REALISE FISHING IS
STUPID AND BORING.

DESMOND TUTU

MY TWO FAVOURITE
THINGS IN LIFE
ARE LIBRARIES AND
BICYCLES. THEY BOTH
MOVE PEOPLE FORWARD
WITHOUT WASTING
ANYTHING. THE PERFECT
DAY: RIDING A BIKE TO
THE LIBRARY.

PETER GOLKIN

THERE IS BEAUTY IN SILENCE AND THERE IS SILENCE IN BEAUTY AND YOU CAN FIND BOTH IN A BICYCLE!

MEHMET MURAT ILDAN

YES; BICYCLING'S A CAPITAL THING FOR A LITERARY MAN.

GEORGE BERNARD SHAW

THE BICYCLE SURELY SHOULD ALWAYS BE THE VEHICLE OF NOVELISTS AND POETS.

CHRISTOPHER MORLEY

I THOUGHT
OF THAT WHILE
RIDING
MY BICYCLE.

ALBERT EINSTEIN,
on the Theory of Relativity

MELANCHOLY IS INCOMPATIBLE WITH BICYCLING.

JAMES E. STARRS

WHEN HOPE SEEMS
HARDLY WORTH
HAVING, JUST
MOUNT A BICYCLE
AND GO OUT FOR
A SPIN DOWN
THE ROAD.

SIR ARTHUR
CONAN DOYLE,
1896

THE BICYCLE IS
STRONGER THAN
ANXIETY, STRONGER
THAN SADNESS. IT HAS
ALL THE POWER
OF HOPE.

MAURICE LEBLANC,
1898

GOOD
FOR THE
BODY

TOLERATION IS
THE GREATEST GIFT
OF THE MIND; IT
REQUIRES THE SAME
EFFORT OF THE BRAIN
THAT IT TAKES TO
BALANCE ONESELF
ON A BICYCLE.

HELEN KELLER

SINCE THE BICYCLE
CONTRIBUTES LITTLE
TO POLLUTION, MAKES A
POSITIVE CONTRIBUTION
TO HEALTH, AND CAUSES
LITTLE DEATH OR INJURY,
IT CAN BE REGARDED AS
THE MOST BENEVOLENT
OF MACHINES.

S. S. WILSON

RIDE AS MUCH OR AS LITTLE, OR AS LONG OR AS SHORT AS YOU FEEL. BUT RIDE.

EDDY MERCKX

HE NEITHER
DRANK, SMOKED,
NOR RODE A BICYCLE.
HE DIED EARLY,
SURROUNDED BY
GREEDY RELATIVES.
IT WAS A GREAT
LESSON TO ME.

JOHN BARRYMORE

BUY A CYCLE, USE IT WITH DISCRETION AND SECURE HEALTH, HAPPINESS AND LONG LIFE!

W. N. ROBERTSON,
1894

THE BICYCLE IS
ITS OWN BEST
ARGUMENT. YOU
JUST GET ON A
BIKE, TRY IT, START
GOING WITH THE
THING AND USING
IT AS IT SUITS YOU.

RICHARD BALLANTINE

RACING

IF YOU USE YOUR BRAKES, YOU DON'T WIN.

MARIO CIPOLLINI

WHEN MY LEGS HURT, I SAY, 'SHUT UP LEGS! DO WHAT I TELL YOU TO DO!'

JENS VOIGT

THE LESS MACHINE THERE IS THE BETTER.

GRAEME OBREE

I RACE TO WIN, NOT TO PLEASE PEOPLE.

BERNARD HINAULT

HERE'S THE
ROUTINE I'D ADVISE
FOR THE EVENING
BEFORE A RACE:
A PHEASANT WITH
CHESTNUTS,
A BOTTLE OF
CHAMPAGNE AND
A WOMAN.

JACQUES ANQUETIL

I'LL TELL YOU SOMETHING ABOUT CYCLING. WE'RE A BUNCH OF WOMEN. GOSSIPY WOMEN.

MARK CAVENDISH

IF YOU CONCENTRATE
ON MAKING MONEY
YOU'LL LOSE RACES;
IF YOU CONCENTRATE
ON WINNING RACES
YOU'LL MAKE MONEY.

ALEX VIROT

PROFESSIONAL CYCLING IS A BIT OF A RAT RACE, BUT IF I'M ONE OF THE TOP RATS I CAN BEAR IT.

TOM SIMPSON

WHEN YOU WIN
SPRINTS YOU PROVE
YOU'RE A GREAT
SPRINTER. WHEN YOU
WIN A GREAT ONE-DAY
RACE, YOU'VE PROVED
YOU'RE A GREAT RIDER.

MARK CAVENDISH

THE RACE IS ALL ABOUT SURVIVING, SURVIVING, SURVIVING.

TOM BOONEN

IN CYCLING, YOU CAN PUT ALL YOUR MONEY ON ONE HORSE.

STEPHEN ROCHE

CLARITY IS SOMETHING
THAT YOU DON'T
OFTEN HAVE AS A
CYCLIST: DECISIONS
ARE CLOUDED BY THE
DESIRE TO PERFORM,
AND THEN ARE LOST IN
THE FOG OF FATIGUE.

CHARLY WEGELIUS

THE FRONT WHEEL CROSSES THE FINISH LINE, CLOSELY FOLLOWED BY THE BACK WHEEL.

HUGH PORTER

TOUR DE
FRANCE

IT'S NICE TO BE
RECOGNISED
FOR ACHIEVING
SOMETHING IN LIFE
BECAUSE SO MUCH
IS BUILT ON PEOPLE
BEING FAMOUS FOR
NOT ACHIEVING
ANYTHING.

BRADLEY WIGGINS

WHEN I SEE POT-BELLIED CYCLISTS WEARING THE MAILLOT JAUNE, IT APPALS ME.

BERNARD HINAULT

YOU HAVE NO IDEA WHAT THE TOUR DE FRANCE IS. IT'S A CALVARY.

HENRI PÉLISSIER,
1914

PUT ME BACK ON MY BIKE.

TOM SIMPSON,
just before he died

WHENEVER SOMEONE WAVED A FLAG, MERCKX WOULD SPRINT FOR IT.

BARRY HOBAN

WITH THE END OF THE TOUR DE FRANCE THE SUMMER REACHES ITS MOMENT OF SADNESS.

PAUL FOURNEL

THE RACE IS ALWAYS
WON BY A STRONG
MAN. THE TRUTH
COMES THROUGH
THE PEDALS.

LAURENT JALABERT

THIS IS A PEDIGREE GROUP OF MEN – THEY ARE HOLDING ON BY THE SKIN OF THEIR SHORTS.

PHIL LIGGETT

LOOKING
GOOD

THE DAY I STOP RIDING MY BIKE FOR A LIVING IS THE DAY I STOP SHAVING MY LEGS. FACT.

MARK CAVENDISH

THE LABOUR IS CONSIDERABLE, AND THE CHAFING EXCESSIVE.

REV GEORGE HERBERT

UNLESS ANYONE
IS POSSESSED OF
LEGS OF IRON AND
THIGHS OF BRASS,
I WOULD STRONGLY
RECOMMEND HIM
TO LOOK BEFORE
HE LEAPS INTO THE
SADDLE OF
A BICYCLE.

ENGLISH MECHANIC,
1899

THERE WAS NO WAY I WAS GOING TO GET MARRIED WITH SHAVED LEGS IN A KILT.

GRAEME OBREE

HE'S DANCING ON HIS PEDALS IN A MOST IMMODEST WAY!

PHIL LIGGETT

I HAVE CYCLING FRIENDS I SEE ONLY ON THE BIKE. I WOULDN'T RECOGNISE THEM IN A SUIT AND TIE.

PAUL FOURNEL

DON'T GO TO CHURCH IN YOUR BICYCLE COSTUME.

NEW YORK WORLD,
1895

DIET (AND SUPPLEMENTS)

DIET? NO FOULER SWEARWORD CAN BE SAID IN MY HOUSE.

JACQUES ANQUETIL

YOU CANNOT COMPETE IN THE TOUR DE FRANCE ON MINERAL WATER ALONE.

JACQUES ANQUETIL

NOTHING
REQUIRES
A CLEAR HEAD,
A STEADY HAND
AND UNSHAKEN
NERVES MORE
THAN CYCLING.

DR VICTOR NEESEN,
1872

LOVE
ON A
BICYCLE

BICYCLES ARE ALMOST AS GOOD AS GUITARS FOR MEETING GIRLS.

BOB WEIR

RIDING A BICYCLE
MAKES YOU IMPOTENT.
THAT'S WHY I CARRY
A BICYCLE SEAT
IN MY POCKET.
IT'S BETTER THAN
WEARING A CONDOM.

JAROD KINTZ

A BRITISH
TRICYCLER NAMED
CHOLMONDELY

ONCE WOOED
A TRICYCLERESS
COLMONDELY

SHE FROWNED
AT HIS SUIT

AND TOLD HIM
TO SCOOT

WHICH REPLY
HE RECEIVED
GLOLMONDELY.

WHEELING ANNUAL,
1881

DAISY, DAISY, GIVE ME
YOUR ANSWER, DO!

I'M HALF CRAZY ALL FOR
THE LOVE OF YOU!

IT WON'T BE A STYLISH
MARRIAGE,

I CAN'T AFFORD A
CARRIAGE,

BUT YOU'LL LOOK SWEET
UPON THE SEAT

OF A BICYCLE BUILT
FOR TWO!

HARRY DACRE,
1892

WHEN I WAS WINNING I PERMITTED MYSELF ONE SEXUAL ENCOUNTER A YEAR.

ALFREDO BINDA

MARRIAGE IS A WONDERFUL INVENTION; BUT THEN AGAIN, SO IS A BICYCLE REPAIR KIT.

BILLY CONNOLLY

YOUR WIFE IS YOUR BICYCLE.

ALPHONSE BAUGÉ

BICYCLE RIDING AS LITTLE AS THREE MILES A DAY WILL IMPROVE YOUR SEX LIFE.

DR FRANCO ANTONINI

CYCLING TO
FREEDOM

BICYCLES HAVE NO WALLS.

PAUL CORNISH

A BICYCLE RIDE AROUND THE WORLD BEGINS WITH A SINGLE PEDAL STROKE.

SCOTT STOLL

BICYCLING IS
THE NEAREST
APPROXIMATION I
KNOW TO THE FLIGHT
OF BIRDS. THE AIRPLANE
SIMPLY CARRIES A MAN
ON HIS BACK LIKE AN
OBEDIENT PEGASUS.

LOUIS J. HELLE JNR

ON A BICYCLE YOU FEEL A DIFFERENT PERSON; YOU FORGET WHO YOU ARE.

DOROTHY RICHARDSON

GOD CREATED THE BICYCLE FOR MEN TO USE AS AN INSTRUMENT OF EFFORT AND EXALTATION ON THE HARD ROAD OF LIFE.

Inscription on bust of Fausto Coppi in the
cyclists' chapel, Madonna del Ghisallo

IT WAS LIKE A NEW
LIFE STARTING UP,
AS IF TILL THEN I'D
BEEN TIED BY A
MILE-LONG ROPE
ROUND THE ANKLE
TO HOME.

ALAN SILLITOE

I WON! I WON! I DON'T HAVE TO GO TO SCHOOL ANY MORE!

EDDY MERCKX

CYCLING CAN BE LONELY, BUT IN A GOOD WAY.

DAVID BYRNE

CYCLING IS THE MOST POPULAR SPORT BECAUSE YOU DON'T HAVE TO PAY FOR THE TICKET.

PIER PAOLO PASOLINI

ACCIDENTS

NEVER USE YOUR FACE AS A BRAKE PAD.

JAKE WATSON

TRUTH HURTS. MAYBE NOT AS MUCH AS JUMPING ON A BICYCLE WITH A SEAT MISSING, BUT IT HURTS.

LESLIE NIELSEN

THERE MAY BE A
BETTER LAND WHERE
SADDLES ARE MADE
OUT OF RAINBOW,
STUFFED WITH CLOUD;
IN THIS WORLD THE
SIMPLEST THING IS
TO GET USED TO
SOMETHING HARD.

JEROME K. JEROME,
1900

WHAT DO YOU CALL A CYCLIST WHO DOESN'T WEAR A HELMET? AN ORGAN DONOR.

DAVID BERRY

THE SOUND OF A CAR DOOR OPENING IN FRONT OF YOU IS SIMILAR TO THE SOUND OF A GUN BEING COCKED.

AMY WEBSTER

OH, TO JUST GRIP
YOUR HANDLEBARS
AND GO RIPPING AND
TEARING THROUGH
STREETS, WONDERING
ALL THE TIME WHEN
YOU'RE GOING TO
SMASH UP.

JACK LONDON

HE WENT FOR A
PEACEABLE ROLL;

HIS WHEEL TOOK A
PIECE OF A HOLE,

AND IT SOON
CAME TO PASS

THAT A REQUIEM MASS

WAS SUNG FOR THE
PEACE OF HIS SOUL.

S. CONANT FOSTER,
1884

THE PROBLEM IS THAT YOU CAN BE WOUNDED IN YOUR MIND AS WELL AS YOUR PHYSIQUE.

MARCO PANTANI

WHO AM I?
WHERE AM I?
OH YES, I'M AT THE TOUR
SO I SHOULD GET ON
MY BIKE AND GO.

DJAMOLIDIN ABDOUJAPAROV,
just after a crash, 1966

PAIN

YOU DON'T SUFFER, KILL YOURSELF AND TAKE THE RISKS I TAKE JUST FOR MONEY. I LOVE BIKE RACING.

GREG LEMOND

IT'S LIKE HOLDING
YOUR HAND IN THE FIRE.
IT'S A CASE OF WHO
CAN DEAL WITH THE
PAIN THE LONGEST.

GRAEME OBREE

IT NEVER
GETS EASIER, YOU
JUST GO FASTER.

GREG LEMOND

THE GREATER
THE SUFFERING,
THE GREATER
THE PLEASURE.

TIM KRABBÉ

THE AMOUNT
OF PAIN THAT A
PROFESSIONAL CYCLIST
GOES THROUGH
FAR EXCEEDS WHAT
MOST PEOPLE WOULD
EXPERIENCE IN THEIR
ENTIRE LIVES.

CHARLY WEGELIUS

CYCLING ISN'T A GAME, IT'S A SPORT. TOUGH, HARD AND UNPITYING.

JEAN DE GRIBALDY

POLITICS

I LIKE RIDING
A BICYCLE BUILT FOR
TWO – BY MYSELF.

HARRY S. TRUMAN

THE PLACE OF CYCLING IN OUR SOCIETY IS SET TO GROW, AND I AM COMMITTED TO DOING EVERYTHING POSSIBLE TO ENCOURAGE THAT.

GORDON BROWN

EVERY TIME I SEE AN
ADULT ON A BICYCLE,
I NO LONGER DESPAIR
FOR THE FUTURE OF
THE HUMAN RACE.

H. G. WELLS

SOCIALISM CAN ONLY ARRIVE BY BICYCLE.

JOSÉ ANTONIO
VIERA-GALLO

ON EVERY REAL BICYCLE THERE IS THE BANNER OF FREEDOM.

WILLIAM FITZWATER

THE BICYCLE
IS A VEHICLE FOR
REVOLUTION.

DANIEL BEHRMAN

I GREW UP IN
THE '30S WITH AN
UNEMPLOYED FATHER.
HE DIDN'T RIOT. HE
GOT ON HIS BIKE AND
LOOKED FOR WORK.

NORMAN TEBBIT

YOU CANNOT BE FOR A START-UP, HIGH-TECH ECONOMY AND NOT BE PRO-BIKE.

RAHM EMANUEL

SUCH HISTORIANS
AS RECORD THE TIDES
OF SOCIAL MANNERS
AND MORALS, HAVE
NEGLECTED THE
BICYCLE.

JOHN GALSWORTHY,
1930

IN THE
SADDLE

WIND IS JUST A HILL IN GASEOUS FORM.

BARRY MCCARTY

IF THE WIND IS NOT AGAINST YOU, IT IS NOT BLOWING.

JAMES E. STARRS

AFTER YOUR FIRST
DAY OF CYCLING,
A MEMORY OF
MOTION LINGERS
IN THE MUSCLES OF
YOUR LEGS, AND
ROUND AND ROUND
THEY SEEM TO GO.

H. G. WELLS

MOVING THE LEGS
EVENLY AND STEADILY
BRINGS HOME A
SENSIBLE RESPECT
FOR TIMING AND
THE MEETING OF
A SCHEDULE.

WILLIAM SAROYAN

NOW I'M OLDER,
THERE'S NO
LONGER A DIRECT
CORRELATION
BETWEEN MY
FITNESS AND
ENJOYMENT ON
THE BIKE.

DAVID MILLAR

MECHANICS

I RELAX BY
TAKING MY BICYCLE
APART AND PUTTING
IT BACK TOGETHER
AGAIN.

MICHELLE PFEIFFER

BICYCLE RIDING, IF GONE IN FOR TO ANY GREAT EXTENT, RESULTS IN DEPRESSION.

ENGLISH MECHANIC,
c1900

THE BICYCLE WAS THE LAST ADVANCE IN TECHNOLOGY EVERYBODY UNDERSTANDS.

STEWART PARKER

I DESIGNED
AND BUILT MY OWN
BIKE FOR ABOUT £70,
BEGGING SPARE PARTS
FROM BIKE SHOPS AND
USING BITS OF AN OLD
WASHING MACHINE.

GRAEME OBREE

YOU HAVE TO BALANCE YOUR SYSTEM MORE CAREFULLY THAN YOU EVER DID YOUR ACCOUNTS.

FRANCES E. WILLARD

THERE ARE TWO WAYS YOU CAN GET EXERCISE OUT OF A BICYCLE. YOU CAN OVERHAUL IT, OR YOU CAN RIDE IT.

JEROME K. JEROME, 1900

CYCLING IS THE
MAN-MACHINE. IT'S
ABOUT DYNAMICS,
CONTINUING
STRAIGHT AHEAD,
FORWARDS, NO
STOPPING. HE WHO
STOPS FALLS OVER.
ALWAYS FORWARD.

RALF HÜTTER

BIKISH CHAOS GRATIFIES THAT INSTINCT, WHICH IS COMMON TO ALL STUPID PEOPLE, THE INSTINCT TO POTTER WITH MACHINERY.

MAX BEERBOHM

SUBSTANTIAL
WEIGHT IS A RELIABLE
MEASURE OF HIGH
QUALITY. THE TWO
EXCEPTIONS TO THIS
RULE ARE BICYCLES
AND WOMEN.

UNKNOWN

CYCLING'S EVERLASTING APPEAL

BICYCLES MAY CHANGE, BUT CYCLING IS TIMELESS.

ZAPATA ESPINOZA

I'M LAZY. BUT IT'S THE LAZY PEOPLE WHO INVENTED THE WHEEL AND THE BICYCLE BECAUSE THEY DIDN'T LIKE WALKING OR CARRYING THINGS.

LECH WALESA

WHOEVER INVENTED THE BICYCLE DESERVES THE THANKS OF HUMANITY.

LORD CHARLES
BERESFORD

NOTHING COMPARES TO THE SIMPLE PLEASURE OF A BIKE RIDE.

JOHN F. KENNEDY

EVER BIKE? NOW THAT'S SOMETHING THAT MAKES LIFE WORTH LIVING.

JACK LONDON

IT IS THE UNKNOWN AROUND THE CORNER THAT TURNS MY WHEELS.

HEINZ STÜCKE

IF I CAN BICYCLE, I BICYCLE.

DAVID ATTENBOROUGH

BIKES
AT WAR

ON THE VERY LAST DAY
OF THE MANOEUVRES
2ND LT CLARK MET WITH A
VERY SERIOUS ACCIDENT
IN CONSEQUENCE OF
HIS SWORD BECOMING
ENTANGLED IN
THE CYCLE.

MAJOR GENERAL F. MAURICE,
Report on Cycle Manœuvres in
Brighton District, 1900

A BIKE,
A BIKE! MY KINGDOM
FOR A BIKE!

ROBERT BLATCHFORD

A CYCLIST, STANDING
WITH HIS CYCLE, WITH
RIFLE ATTACHED TO IT,
WILL SALUTE WITH THE
RIGHT HAND, AS LAID
DOWN IN SECTION
19, RETURNING THE
HAND TO THE POINT OF
THE SADDLE ON THE
COMPLETION OF
THE SALUTE.

REGULATION 64,
Army Council manual

OBJECTS
OF DESIRE

WHY SHOULD ANYONE STEAL A WATCH WHEN HE COULD STEAL A BICYCLE?

FLANN O'BRIEN

THINK OF BICYCLES AS RIDEABLE ART THAT CAN JUST ABOUT SAVE THE WORLD.

GRANT PETERSEN

I NEVER WANT TO ABANDON MY BIKE.

STEPHEN ROCHE

THE BICYCLE HAS
A SOUL. IF YOU SUCCEED
TO LOVE IT, IT WILL
GIVE YOU EMOTIONS
THAT YOU WILL
NEVER FORGET.

MARIO CIPOLLINI

COMPANION IN MY
SOLITUDE,

REFUGE WHEN
GLOOMY THOUGHTS
INTRUDE,

MY BICYCLE TO
YOU I SING!

CYCLING MAGAZINE,
1896

IN LIFE'S ORCHESTRA, THE BIKE IS THE DOUBLE BASS. HARD TO FORGET IT.

PAUL FOURNEL

IN ITALY, THE BICYCLE BELONGS TO THE NATIONAL ART HERITAGE IN THE SAME WAY AS MONA LISA, THE DOME OF ST PETER OR THE DIVINE COMEDY.

CURZIO MALAPARTE

I FELT I HAD KNOWN
MY BICYCLE FOR MANY
YEARS AND THAT SHE HAD
KNOWN ME – AND THAT WE
UNDERSTOOD EACH OTHER
UTTERLY.

FLANN O'BRIEN

CODE OF
CYCLISTS

THERE SHOULD
BE SOME FORMAL
SALUTATION FOR
THE ROAD, ONE FOR
ENCOURAGEMENT
FOR THE BICYCLIST
GOING UP HILL, ONE
FOR CONGRATULATION
TO THE FORTUNATE
BROTHER GOING
DOWN.

HENRY CHARLES BEECHING,
1899

I HAD AN EARLY
ACCIDENT WITH MY
NEW BICYCLE WHEN,
IN TAKING MY ARM
FROM THE HANDLEBAR
IN ORDER TO RAISE MY
HAT TO A LADY, I RODE
INTO A LAMP POST.

COMPTON MCKENZIE

NOTHING HISSES QUITE SO SWEETLY AS A RIVAL'S PUNCTURE.

TIM KRABBÉ

THERE IS ALWAYS
UNPLEASANTNESS
ABOUT THIS TANDEM.
IT IS THE THEORY OF THE
MAN IN FRONT THAT
THE MAN BEHIND DOES
NOTHING; IT IS EQUALLY
THE THEORY OF THE MAN
BEHIND THAT HE ALONE
IS THE MOTIVE POWER,
THE MAN IN FRONT
MERELY DOING THE
PUFFING. THE MYSTERY
WILL NEVER BE SOLVED.

JEROME K. JEROME,
1900

REFRAIN FROM THROWING YOUR BICYCLE IN PUBLIC. IT SHOWS POOR UPBRINGING.

JACQUIE PHELAN

PERILS

A GIRL, OR INDEED ANY WOMAN, RIDING ALONE MUST BE IN SOME CONSIDERABLE PERIL.

MRS HARCOURT
WILLIAMSON,
1897

THERE IS A CERTAIN
TYPE OF DRIVER IN
NEW YORK WHO
LIKES TO WATCH
IN HIS REAR VIEW
MIRROR FOR A
CYCLIST. HERE
COMES ONE NOW!
TIME TO OPEN THE
FRONT DOOR...

NEW YORKER MAGAZINE

IT'S ONE OF THE WORST THINGS IN THE WORLD TO WAKE UP AND NOT SEE YOUR BIKE WHERE YOU LEFT IT.

50 CENT

I BELIEVE CARS ARE THE NEW SECOND-HAND SMOKE.

DAVE ZABRISKIE

I CYCLE ON THE BASIS THAT EVERYONE IS OUT TO KILL YOU.

JON SNOW

IF YOU RIDE YOUR BIKE,
YOU MIGHT GET HURT,
YOU MIGHT BECOME
IMPOTENT, AND, HELL,
YOU MIGHT EVEN DIE.
WHAT TO DO?
RIDE YOUR BIKE
ANYWAY.

ZAPATA ESPINOZA

TRAINING

IF THE TRAINING IS HARD, THE RACING IS EASY.

EDDY MERCKX

RIDE YOUR BIKE, RIDE YOUR BIKE, RIDE YOUR BIKE.

FAUSTO COPPI

A RIDER SAYS TO ME, 'I GO OUT TRAINING TWO HOURS EVERY MORNING.' BUT I ASK HIM, 'WHAT ABOUT THE AFTERNOON?'

SEAN KELLY

25,000 PEOPLE
SHOW UP TO START
A MARATHON IN
NEW YORK. ONLY 200
PEOPLE CAN START
THE TOUR
DE FRANCE.

GREG LEMOND

GOOD MORALE IN CYCLING COMES FROM GOOD LEGS.

SEAN YATES

THE
MOUNTAINS

A GOOD RIDER IS
INTUITIVE. YOU CAN
LOOK AT OTHER
CYCLISTS AND KNOW
JUST HOW GOOD THEY
ARE BY HOW THEY
PEDAL OR BREATHE.

THURLOW ROGERS

IT'S REALLY
SOMETHING TO SEE,
A CLIMBER WAITING
TO ATTACK. ANY
OTHER SORT OF
ATTACK CAN BE
NEUTRALISED, BUT
WHEN A CLIMBER
GOES THERE'S LITTLE
THE NON-CLIMBERS
CAN DO.

RALPH HURNE

YOU DON'T HAVE TO BE MAD TO GO UP THE VENTOUX, BUT YOU'RE MAD IF YOU GO BACK.

PROVENÇAL PROVERB

YOU CAN SAY THAT CLIMBERS SUFFER THE SAME AS THE OTHER RIDERS, BUT THEY SUFFER IN A DIFFERENT WAY. YOU FEEL THE PAIN, BUT YOU'RE GLAD TO BE THERE.

RICHARD VIRENQUE

RIDING A BIKE UP THE GALIBIER IS NOT A NORMAL ACTIVITY.

GEOFFREY WHEATCROFT

THE BICYCLE, IN
THE HANDS OF
A NOVICE, IS AS
ACUTE AS A SPIRIT
LEVEL. IT NOTICES
A RISE WHERE YOUR
UNTRAINED EYE
WOULD NOT KNOW
ONE EXISTED.

MARK TWAIN

BICYCLING
TO A BETTER
TOMORROW

BICYCLING IS A BIG
PART OF THE FUTURE.
IT HAS TO BE. THERE'S
SOMETHING WRONG
WITH A SOCIETY
THAT DRIVES A CAR
TO WORK OUT
IN A GYM.

BILL NYE

BICYCLES ARE THE INDICATOR SPECIES OF A COMMUNITY, LIKE SHELLFISH IN A BAY.

P. MARTIN SCOTT

AN AUTOMOBILE IS EXPENSIVE. YOU HAVE TO FIND A PLACE TO PARK AND IT'S NOT FUN.

STEPHEN G. BREYER

THE BICYCLE IS THE MOST CIVILIZED CONVEYANCE KNOWN TO MAN.

IRIS MURDOCH

CYCLE TRACKS WILL ABOUND IN UTOPIA.

H. G. WELLS

THE BEST USE OF A BICYCLE IS COMMUTING, AND GETTING CARS OFF THE ROADS.

GRANT PETERSEN

NO HOUR
OF LIFE IS LOST
THAT IS SPENT IN
THE SADDLE.

WINSTON CHURCHILL